This book
belongs to:

_____

PSALMS

An All-Day, Every Day Devotional

FaithPoint™
PRESS

Psalms 24/7
An All-Day, Every Day Devotional

Copyright © 2005 by FaithPoint Press

Produced by Cliff Road Books

ISBN: 1-58173-475-1

Book design by Pat Covert

Printed in China

PSALMS

An All-Day, Every Day Devotional

JANUARY 1

Morning: You crown the year with your bounty, and your carts overflow with abundance.

Psalm 65:11

Evening: My shield is God Most High, who saves the upright in heart.

Psalm 7:10

JANUARY 2

Morning: You say, "I choose the appointed time; it is I who judge uprightly."

Psalm 75:2

Evening: But those who turn to crooked ways the LORD will banish with the evildoers. Peace be upon Israel.

Psalm 125:5

JANUARY 3

Morning: Praise him with tambourine and dancing, praise him with the strings and flute.

Psalm 150:4

Evening: My heart is not proud, O LORD, my eyes are not haughty; I do not concern myself with great matters or things too wonderful for me.

Psalm 131:1

JANUARY 4

Morning: I praise you because I am fearfully and wonderfully made; your works are wonderful, I know that full well.

Psalm 139:14

Evening: To you, O LORD, I lift up my soul.

Psalm 25:1

JANUARY 5

Morning: He will defend the afflicted among the people and save the children of the needy; he will crush the oppressor.

Psalm 72:4

Evening: He remembers his covenant forever, the word he commanded, for a thousand generations.

Psalm 105:8

JANUARY 6

Morning: From the ends of the earth I call to you, I call as my heart grows faint; lead me to the rock that is higher than I.

Psalm 61:2

Evening: I will sing of your love and justice; to you, O LORD, I will sing praise.

Psalm 101:1

JANUARY 7

Morning: He brought out his people with rejoicing, his chosen ones with shouts of joy.

Psalm 105:43

Evening: It is good to praise the LORD and make music to your name, O Most High.

Psalm 92:1

JANUARY 8

Morning: With my mouth I will greatly extol the LORD; in the great throng I will praise him.

Psalm 109:30

Evening: Rejoice in the LORD and be glad, you righteous; sing, all you who are upright in heart!

Psalm 32:11

JANUARY 9

Morning: For as high as the heavens are above the earth, so great is his love for those who fear him.

Psalm 103:11

Evening: He trusts in the LORD; let the LORD rescue him. Let him deliver him, since he delights in him.

Psalm 22:8

JANUARY 10

Morning: In you our fathers put their trust; they trusted and you delivered them.

Psalm 22:4

Evening: LORD, what is man that you care for him, the son of man that you think of him?

Psalm 144:3

JANUARY 11

Morning: Praise the LORD. Sing to the LORD a new song, his praise in the assembly of the saints.

Psalm 149:1

Evening: They will celebrate your abundant goodness and joyfully sing of your righteousness.

Psalm 145:7

JANUARY 12

Morning: Sons are a heritage from the LORD, children a reward from him.

Psalm 127:3

Evening: When I am afraid, I will trust in you.

Psalm 56:3

JANUARY 13

Morning: In your distress you called and I rescued you, I answered you out of a thundercloud; I
tested you at the waters of Meribah. Selah

Psalm 81:7

Evening: The LORD Almighty is with us; the God of Jacob is our fortress.

Psalm 46:11

JANUARY 14

Morning: Praise the LORD, all his works everywhere in his dominion. Praise the LORD, O my soul.

Psalm 103:22

Evening: Rejoice in the LORD, you who are righteous, and praise his holy name.

Psalm 97:12

JANUARY 15

Morning: For he knows how we are formed, he remembers that we are dust.

Psalms 103:14

Evening: Then men will say, "Surely the righteous still are rewarded; surely there is a God who judges the earth."

Psalm 58:11

JANUARY 16

Morning: Hear my prayer, O God; listen to the words of my mouth.

Psalm 54:2

Evening: I will praise God's name in song and glorify him with thanksgiving.

Psalm 69:30

JANUARY 17

Morning: You are awesome, O God, in your sanctuary; the God of Israel gives power and strength to his people.

Psalm 68:35

Evening: Do not hold against us the sins of the fathers; may your mercy come quickly to meet us, for we are in desperate need.

Psalm 79:8

JANUARY 18

Morning: Let everything that has breath praise the LORD. Praise the LORD.

Psalm 150:6

Evening: Clap your hands, all you nations; shout to God with cries of joy.

Psalm 47:1

JANUARY 19

Morning: Look to the LORD and his strength; seek his face always.

Psalm 105:4

Evening: The LORD is gracious and righteous; our God is full of compassion.

Psalm 116:5

JANUARY 20

Morning: Listen to my prayer, O God, do not ignore my plea.

Psalm 55:1

Evening: I will say of the LORD, "He is my refuge and my fortress, my God, in whom I trust."

Psalm 91:2

JANUARY 21

Morning: Delight yourself in the LORD and he will give you the desires of your heart.

Psalm 37:4

Evening: The eyes of the LORD are on the righteous and his ears are attentive to their cry.

Psalm 34:15

JANUARY 22

Morning: Your throne, O God, will last for ever and ever; a scepter of justice will be the scepter of your kingdom.

Psalm 45:6

Evening: How lovely is your dwelling place, O LORD Almighty!

Psalm 84:1

JANUARY 23

Morning: I cry out to God Most High, to God, who fulfills [his purpose] for me.

Psalm 57:2

Evening: But you, O LORD, be not far off; O my Strength, come quickly to help me.

Psalm 22:19

JANUARY 24

Morning: Satisfy us in the morning with your unfailing love, that we may sing for joy and be glad all our days.

Psalm 90:14

Evening: Surely God is my help; the LORD is the one who sustains me.

Psalm 54:4

JANUARY 25

Morning: May the nations be glad and sing for joy, for you rule the peoples justly and guide the nations of the earth. Selah

Psalm 67:4

Evening: Defend the cause of the weak and fatherless; maintain the rights of the poor and oppressed.

Psalm 82:3

JANUARY 26

Morning: He upholds the cause of the oppressed and gives food to the hungry. The LORD sets prisoners free.

Psalm 146:7

Evening: Wash away all my iniquity and cleanse me from my sin.

Psalm 51:2

JANUARY 27

Morning: The highest heavens belong to the LORD, but the earth he has given to man.

Psalm 116:16

Evening: Hear my prayer, O LORD; let my cry for help come to you.

Psalm 102:1

JANUARY 28

Morning: Praise be to the LORD God, the God of Israel, who alone does marvelous deeds.

Psalm 72:18

Evening: Worship the LORD with gladness; come before him with joyful songs.

Psalm 100:2

JANUARY 29

Morning: Have mercy on us, O LORD, have mercy on us, for we have endured much contempt.

Psalm 123:3

Evening: O LORD, our LORD, how majestic is your name in all the earth!

Psalm 8:9

JANUARY 30

Morning: Praise the LORD, you his angels, you mighty ones who do his bidding, who obey his word.

Psalm 103:20

Evening: Let the righteous rejoice in the LORD and take refuge in him; let all the upright in heart praise him!

Psalm 64:10

JANUARY 31

Morning: I spread out my hands to you; my soul thirsts for you like a parched land. Selah

Psalm 143:6

Evening: Do not hide your face from me when I am in distress. Turn your ear to me; when I call, answer me quickly.

Psalm 102:2

FEBRUARY 1

Morning: Hear, O LORD, and answer me, for I am poor and needy.

Psalm 86:1

Evening: Praise the LORD, all his heavenly hosts, you his servants who do his will.

Psalm 103:21

FEBRUARY 2

Morning: O God, you are my God, earnestly I seek you; my soul thirsts for you, my body longs for you, in a dry and weary land where there is no water.

Psalm 62:1

Evening: Hear me and answer me. My thoughts trouble me and I am distraught.

Psalm 55:2

FEBRUARY 3

Morning: Exalt the LORD our God and worship at his holy mountain, for the LORD our God is holy.

Psalm 99:9

Evening: Hear me, O God, as I voice my complaint; protect my life from the threat of the enemy.

Psalm 64:1

FEBRUARY 4

Morning: Say to God, "How awesome are your deeds! So great is your power that your enemies cringe before you."

Psalm 66:3

Evening: Guard my life, for I am devoted to you. You are my God; save your servant who trusts in you.

Psalm 86:2

FEBRUARY 5

Morning: Worship the LORD in the splendor of his holiness; tremble before him, all the earth.

Psalm 96:9

Evening: For you, O LORD, have delivered my soul from death, my eyes from tears, my feet from stumbling.

Psalm 116:8

FEBRUARY 6

Morning: Save me, for I am yours; I have sought out your precepts.

Psalm 119:94

Evening: I will declare your name to my brothers; in the congregation I will praise you.

Psalm 22:22

FEBRUARY 7

Morning: Hear my prayer, O LORD God Almighty; listen to me, O God of Jacob. Selah

Psalm 84:8

Evening: Cast your cares on the LORD and he will sustain you; he will never let the righteous fall.

Psalm 55:22

FEBRUARY 8

Morning: Show us your unfailing love, O LORD, and grant us your salvation.

Psalm 85:7

Evening: May the peoples praise you, O God; may all the peoples praise you.

Psalm 67:5

FEBRUARY 9

Morning: I cried out to God for help; I cried out to God to hear me.

Psalm 77:1

Evening: He alone is my rock and my salvation; he is my fortress, I will never be shaken.

Psalm 62:2

FEBRUARY 10

Morning: O LORD God Almighty, who is like you? You are mighty, O LORD, and your faithfulness surrounds you.

Psalm 89:8

Evening: Deliver me from my enemies, O God; protect me from those who rise up against me.

Psalm 59:1

FEBRUARY 11

Morning: As for me, I will declare this forever; I will sing praise to the God of Jacob.

Psalm 75:9

Evening: Our God is a God who saves; from the Sovereign LORD comes escape from death.

Psalm 68:20

FEBRUARY 12

Morning: Sing joyfully to the LORD, you righteous; it is fitting for the upright to praise him.

Psalm 33:1

Evening: Refrain from anger and turn from wrath; do not fret—it leads only to evil.

Psalm 37:8

FEBRUARY 13

Morning: The LORD sustains the humble but casts the wicked to the ground.

Psalm 147:6

Evening: He makes wars cease to the ends of the earth; he breaks the bow and shatters the spear, he burns the shields with fire.

Psalm 46:9

FEBRUARY 14

Morning: Because your love is better than life, my lips will glorify you.

Psalm 62:3

Evening: In you, O LORD, I have taken refuge; let me never be put to shame; deliver me in your righteousness.

Psalm 31:1

FEBRUARY 15

Morning: Know that the LORD is God. It is he who made us, and we are his; we are his people, the sheep of his pasture.

Psalm 100:3

Evening: I will praise you, O LORD, among the nations; I will sing of you among the peoples.

Psalm 57:9

FEBRUARY 16

Morning: Teach me your way, O LORD, and I will walk in your truth; give me an undivided heart, that I may fear your name.

Psalm 86:11

Evening: All kings will bow down to him and all nations will serve him.

Psalm 72:11

FEBRUARY 17

Morning: But I call to God, and the LORD saves me.

Psalm 55:16

Evening: A righteous man may have many troubles, but the LORD delivers him from them all.

Psalm 34:19

FEBRUARY 18

Morning: Sing to the LORD, you saints of his; praise his holy name.

Psalm 30:4

Evening: Whoever is wise, let him heed these things and consider the great love of the LORD.

Psalm 107:43

FEBRUARY 19

Morning: Have mercy on me, O God, according to your unfailing love; according to your great compassion blot out my transgressions.

Psalm 51:1

Evening: In vain you rise early and stay up late, toiling for food to eat—for he grants sleep to those he loves.

Psalm 127:2

FEBRUARY 20

Morning: For he will deliver the needy who cry out, the afflicted who have no one to help.

Psalm 72:12

Evening: Do not withhold your mercy from me, O LORD; may your love and your truth always protect me.

Psalm 40:11

FEBRUARY 21

Morning: I will praise you, O LORD my God, with all my heart; I will glorify your name forever.

Psalm 86:12

Evening: The LORD does whatever pleases him, in the heavens and on the earth, in the seas and all their depths.

Psalm 135:6

FEBRUARY 22

Morning: Blessed is the man who does not walk in the counsel of the wicked or stand in the way of sinners or sit in the seat of mockers.

Psalm 1:1

Evening: You who fear him, trust in the LORD— he is their help and shield.

Psalm 115:11

FEBRUARY 23

Morning: Let their lying lips be silenced, for with pride and contempt they speak arrogantly against the righteous.

Psalm 31:18

Evening: Turn your ear to me, come quickly to my rescue; be my rock of refuge, a strong fortress to save me.

Psalm 31:2

FEBRUARY 24

Morning: Praise the LORD, O my soul; all my inmost being, praise his holy name.

Psalm 103:1

Evening: Praise be to God, who has not rejected my prayer or withheld his love from me!

Psalm 66:20

FEBRUARY 25

Morning: Trust in the LORD and do good; dwell in the land and enjoy safe pasture.

Psalm 37:3

Evening: Save me, O God, by your name; vindicate me by your might.

Psalm 54:1

FEBRUARY 26

Morning: Save us and help us with your right hand, that those you love may be delivered.

Psalm 60:5

Evening: The salvation of the righteous comes from the LORD; he is their stronghold in time of trouble.

Psalm 37:39

FEBRUARY 27

Morning: Let those who love the LORD hate evil, for he guards the lives of his faithful ones and delivers them from the hand of the wicked.

Psalm 97:10

Evening: In the day of my trouble I will call to you, for you will answer me.

Psalm 86:7

FEBRUARY 28

Morning: Commit your way to the LORD; trust in him and he will do this.

Psalm 37:5

Evening: Great is the LORD, and most worthy of praise, in the city of our God, his holy mountain.

Psalm 48:1

FEBRUARY 29

Morning: Your laws endure to this day, for all things serve you.

Psalm 119:91

Evening: Blessed are they who maintain justice, who constantly do what is right.

Psalm 106:3

MARCH 1

Morning: Unless the LORD builds the house, its builders labor in vain. Unless the LORD watches over the city, the watchmen stand guard in vain.

Psalm 127:1

Evening: I love the house where you live, O LORD, the place where your glory dwells.

Psalm 26:8

MARCH 2

Morning: Let the saints rejoice in this honor and sing for joy on their beds.

Psalm 149:5

Evening: The Mighty One, God, the LORD, speaks and summons the earth from the rising of the sun to the place where it sets.

Psalm 50:1

MARCH 3

Morning: Your love, O LORD, reaches to the heavens, your faithfulness to the skies.

Psalm 36:5

Evening: Answer me when I call to you, O my righteous God. Give me relief from my distress; be merciful to me and hear my prayer.

Psalm 4:1

MARCH 4

Morning: Come, let us sing for joy to the LORD; let us shout aloud to the Rock of our salvation.

Psalm 95:1

Evening: Lead me, O LORD, in your righteousness because of my enemies—make straight your way before me.

Psalm 5:8

MARCH 5

Morning: Hide your face from my sins and blot out all my iniquity.

Psalm 51:9

Evening: The LORD reigns forever; he has established his throne for judgment.

Psalm 9:7

MARCH 6

Morning: The righteous will flourish like a palm tree, they will grow like a cedar of Lebanon.

Psalm 92:12

Evening: He fulfills the desires of those who fear him; he hears their cry and saves them.

Psalm 145:19

MARCH 7

Morning: The LORD has established his throne in heaven, and his kingdom rules over all.

Psalm 103:19

Evening: To the faithful you show yourself faithful, to the blameless you show yourself blameless.

Psalm 18:25

MARCH 8

Morning: The heavens proclaim his righteousness, and all the peoples see his glory.

Psalm 97:6

Evening: Teach me your way, O LORD; lead me in a straight path because of my oppressors.

Psalm 27:11

MARCH 9

Morning: No one who practices deceit will dwell in my house; no one who speaks falsely will stand in my presence.

Psalm 101:7

Evening: Hear, O LORD, and be merciful to me; O LORD, be my help.

Psalm 30:10

MARCH 10

Morning: Then they cried out to the LORD in their trouble, and he brought them out of their distress.

Psalm 107:28

Evening: I will instruct you and teach you in the way you should go; I will counsel you and watch over you.

Psalm 32:8

MARCH 11

Morning: In the morning, O LORD, you hear my voice; in the morning I lay my requests before you and wait in expectation.

Psalm 5:3

Evening: The voice of the LORD is powerful; the voice of the LORD is majestic.

Psalm 29:4

MARCH 12

Morning: I have set the LORD always before me. Because he is at my right hand, I will not be shaken.

Psalm 16:8

Evening: It is better to take refuge in the LORD than to trust in man.

Psalm 118:8

MARCH 13

Morning: Taste and see that the LORD is good; blessed is the man who takes refuge in him.

Psalm 34:8

Evening: My feet stand on level ground; in the great assembly I will praise the LORD.

Psalm 26:12

MARCH 14

Morning: Sing to the LORD a new song, for he has done marvelous things; his right hand and his holy arm have worked salvation for him.

Psalm 98:1

Evening: Do not trust in extortion or take pride in stolen goods; though your riches increase, do not set your heart on them.

Psalm 62:10

MARCH 15

Morning: The LORD is my light and my salvation—whom shall I fear? The LORD is the stronghold of my life—of whom shall I be afraid?

Psalm 27:1

Evening: I wait for you, O LORD; you will answer, O LORD my God.

Psalm 38:15

MARCH 16

Morning: I will lie down and sleep in peace, for you alone, O LORD, make me dwell in safety.

Psalm 4:8

Evening: My soul yearns, even faints, for the courts of the LORD; my heart and my flesh cry out for the living God.

Psalm 84:2

MARCH 17

Morning: I cry aloud to the LORD; I lift up my voice to the LORD for mercy.

Psalm 142:1

Evening: When anxiety was great within me, your consolation brought joy to my soul.

Psalm 94:19

MARCH 18

Morning: The fear of the LORD is pure, enduring forever. The ordinances of the LORD are sure and altogether righteous.

Psalm 19:9

Evening: Blessed are those who have learned to acclaim you, who walk in the light of your presence, O LORD.

Psalm 89:15

MARCH 19

Morning: Blessed is he whose help is the God of Jacob, whose hope is in the LORD his God.

Psalm 146:5

Evening: Turn from evil and do good; seek peace and pursue it.

Psalm 34:14

MARCH 20

Morning: Do not snatch the word of truth from my mouth, for I have put my hope in your laws.

Psalm 119:43

Evening: Therefore let everyone who is godly pray to you while you may be found; surely when the mighty waters rise, they will not reach him.

Psalm 32:6

MARCH 21

Morning: Consider the blameless, observe the upright; there is a future for the man of peace.

Psalm 37:37

Evening: I meditate on your precepts and consider your ways.

Psalm 119:15

MARCH 22

Morning: As the deer pants for streams of water, so my soul pants for you, O God.

Psalm 42:1

Evening: But man, despite his riches, does not endure; he is like the beasts that perish.

Psalm 49:12

MARCH 23

Morning: Yet I am always with you; you hold me by my right hand.

Psalm 73:23

Evening: The works of his hands are faithful and just; all his precepts are trustworthy.

Psalm 111:7

MARCH 24

Morning: Rescue the weak and needy; deliver them from the hand of the wicked.

Psalm 82:4

Evening: You are my hiding place; you will protect me from trouble and surround me with songs of deliverance.

Psalm 32:7

MARCH 25

Morning: Praise the LORD. Blessed is the man who fears the LORD, who finds great delight in his commands.

Psalm 112:1

Evening: Many are the woes of the wicked, but the LORD's unfailing love surrounds the man who trusts in him.

Psalm 32:10

MARCH 26

Morning: The heavens are yours, and yours also the earth; you founded the world and all that is in it.

Psalm 89:11

Evening: Blessed is the man whose sin the LORD does not count against him and in whose spirit is no deceit. Selah

Psalm 32:2

MARCH 27

Morning: Praise the LORD, O my soul, and forget not all his benefits.

Psalm 103:2

Evening: Let heaven and earth praise him, the seas and all that move in them.

Psalm 69:34

MARCH 28

Morning: God is a righteous judge, a God who expresses his wrath every day.

Psalm 7:11

Evening: The days of the blameless are known to the LORD, and their inheritance will endure forever.

Psalm 37:18

MARCH 29

Morning: I will sacrifice a freewill offering to you; I will praise your name, O LORD, for it is good.

Psalm 54:6

Evening: We give thanks to you, O God, we give thanks, for your Name is near; men tell of your wonderful deeds.

Psalm 75:1

MARCH 30

Morning: He who dwells in the shelter of the Most High will rest in the shadow of the Almighty.

Psalm 91:1

Evening: For you created my inmost being; you knit me together in my mother's womb.

Psalm 139:13

MARCH 31

Morning: You are good, and what you do is good; teach me your decrees.

Psalm 119:68

Evening: I know that you are pleased with me, for my enemy does not triumph over me.

Psalm 41:11

APRIL 1

Morning: Create in me a pure heart, O God, and renew a steadfast spirit within me.

Psalm 51:10

Evening: The LORD will indeed give what is good, and our land will yield its harvest.

Psalm 85:12

APRIL 2

Morning: For the LORD is good and his love endures forever; his faithfulness continues through all generations.

Psalm 100:5

Evening: May your unfailing love come to me, O LORD, your salvation according to your promise.

Psalm 119:41

APRIL 3

Morning: My heart is steadfast, O God; I will sing and make music with all my soul.

Psalm 108:1

Evening: Come and see what God has done, how awesome his works in man's behalf!

Psalm 66:5

APRIL 4

Morning: For the sake of my brothers and friends, I will say, "Peace be within you."

Psalm 122:8

Evening: Teach us to number our days aright, that we may gain a heart of wisdom.

Psalm 90:12

APRIL 5

Morning: As the mountains surround Jerusalem, so the LORD surrounds his people both now and forevermore.

Psalm 125:2

Evening: If the LORD delights in a man's way, he makes his steps firm.

Psalm 37:23

APRIL 6

Morning: Better is one day in your courts than a thousand elsewhere; I would rather be a doorkeeper in the house of my God than dwell in the tents of the wicked.

Psalm 84:10

Evening: I waited patiently for the LORD; he turned to me and heard my cry.

Psalm 40:1

APRIL 7

Morning: I will meditate on all your works and consider all your mighty deeds.

Psalm 77:12

Evening: The wicked borrow and do not repay, but the righteous give generously.

Psalm 37:21

APRIL 8

Morning: The LORD is good to all; he has compassion on all he has made.

Psalm 145:9

Evening: I hold fast to your statutes, O LORD; do not let me be put to shame.

Psalm 119:31

APRIL 9

Morning: The LORD has done great things for us, and we are filled with joy.

Psalm 126:3

Evening: O LORD, you have searched me and you know me.

Psalm 139:1

APRIL 10

Morning: Come and listen, all you who fear God; let me tell you what he has done for me.

Psalm 66:16

Evening: For in the day of trouble he will keep me safe in his dwelling; he will hide me in the shelter of his tabernacle and set me high upon a rock.

Psalm 27:5

APRIL 11

Morning: Your word is a lamp to my feet and a light for my path.

Psalm 119:105

Evening: Set a guard over my mouth, O LORD; keep watch over the door of my lips.

Psalm 141:3

APRIL 12

Morning: They will tell of the power of your awesome works, and I will proclaim your great deeds.

Psalm 145:6

Evening: O LORD, I call to you; come quickly to me. Hear my voice when I call to you.

Psalm 141:1

APRIL 13

Morning: The LORD gives sight to the blind, the LORD lifts up those who are bowed down, the LORD loves the righteous.

Psalm 146:8

Evening: Give thanks to the God of heaven. His love endures forever.

Psalm 136:26

APRIL 14

Morning: Praise be to his glorious name forever; may the whole earth be filled with his glory. Amen and Amen.

Psalm 72:19

Evening: Sing the glory of his name; make his praise glorious!

Psalm 66:2

APRIL 15

Morning: I will give you thanks in the great assembly; among throngs of people I will praise you.

Psalm 35:18

Evening: My heart is steadfast, O God, my heart is steadfast; I will sing and make music.

Psalm 57:7

APRIL 16

Morning: Send forth your light and your truth, let them guide me; let them bring me to your holy mountain, to the place where you dwell.

Psalm 43:3

Evening: But may the righteous be glad and rejoice before God; may they be happy and joyful.

Psalm 68:3

APRIL 17

Morning: Sing for joy to God our strength; shout aloud to the God of Jacob!

Psalm 81:1

Evening: For you are great and do marvelous deeds; you alone are God.

Psalm 86:10

APRIL 18

Morning: Great are the works of the LORD; they are pondered by all who delight in them.

Psalm 111:2

Evening: Blessed are they who keep his statutes and seek him with all their heart.

Psalm 119:2

APRIL 19

Morning: Before a word is on my tongue you know it completely, O LORD.

Psalm 139:4

Evening: I love the LORD, for he heard my voice; he heard my cry for mercy.

Psalm 116:1

APRIL 20

Morning: Great is the LORD and most worthy of praise; his greatness no one can fathom.

Psalm 145:3

Evening: I will exalt you, O LORD, for you lifted me out of the depths and did not let my enemies gloat over me.

Psalm 30:1

APRIL 21

Morning: Nations are in uproar, kingdoms fall; he lifts his voice, the earth melts.

Psalm 46:6

Evening: O LORD my God, I called to you for help and you healed me.

Psalm 30:2

APRIL 22

Morning: O LORD Almighty, blessed is the man who trusts in you.

Psalm 84:12

Evening: You have made known to me the path of life; you will fill me with joy in your presence,
with eternal pleasures at your right hand.

Psalm 16:11

APRIL 23

Morning: For great is his love toward us, and the faithfulness of the LORD endures forever. Praise the LORD.

Psalm 117:2

Evening: For the LORD is the great God, the great King above all gods.

Psalm 95:3

APRIL 24

Morning: My mouth is filled with your praise, declaring your splendor all day long.

Psalm 71:8

Evening: But may all who seek you rejoice and be glad in you; may those who love your salvation always say, "The LORD be exalted!"

Psalm 40:16

APRIL 25

Morning: They will tell of the glory of your kingdom and speak of your might, so that all men may know of your mighty acts and the glorious splendor of your kingdom.

Psalm 145:11-12

Evening: But as for me, I will always have hope; I will praise you more and more.

Psalm 71:14

APRIL 26

Morning: Turn from evil and do good; then you will dwell in the land forever.

Psalm 37:27

Evening: Test me, O LORD, and try me, examine my heart and my mind.

Psalm 26:2

APRIL 27

Morning: O LORD, open my lips, and my mouth will declare your praise.

Psalm 51:15

Evening: No man can redeem the life of another or give to God a ransom for him.

Psalm 49:7

APRIL 28

Morning: For the LORD God is a sun and shield; the LORD bestows favor and honor; no good thing does he withhold from those whose walk is blameless.

Psalm 84:11

Evening: Praise be to the LORD, the God of Israel, from everlasting to everlasting. Let all the people say, "Amen!" Praise the LORD.

Psalm 106:48

APRIL 29

Morning: Enter his gates with thanksgiving and his courts with praise; give thanks to him and praise his name.

Psalm 100:4

Evening: O God, do not keep silent; be not quiet, O God, be not still.

Psalm 83:1

APRIL 30

Morning: Your faithfulness continues through all generations; you established the earth, and it endures.

Psalm 119:90

Evening: How great are your works, O LORD, how profound your thoughts!

Psalm 92:5

MAY 1

Morning: Have mercy on me, O LORD, for I call to you all day long.

Psalm 86:3

Evening: He will judge the world in righteousness; he will govern the peoples with justice.

Psalm 9:8

MAY 2

Morning: Praise the LORD. I will extol the LORD with all my heart in the council of the upright and in the assembly.

Psalm 111:1

Evening: When I said, "My foot is slipping," your love, O LORD, supported me.

Psalm 94:18

MAY 3

Morning: Praise the LORD. Give thanks to the LORD, for he is good; his love endures forever.

Psalm 106:1

Evening: My flesh and my heart may fail, but God is the strength of my heart and my portion forever.

Psalm 73:26

MAY 4

Morning: When my spirit grows faint within me, it is you who know my way. In the path where I walk men have hidden a snare for me.

Psalm 142:3

Evening: Hear my cry, O God; listen to my prayer.

Psalm 61:1

MAY 5

Morning: Praise be to the LORD forever!

Psalm 89:52

Evening: Though the LORD is on high, he looks upon the lowly, but the proud he knows from afar.

Psalm 138:6

MAY 6

Morning: The LORD is my strength and my song; he has become my salvation.

Psalm 118:14

Evening: Sing praises to God, sing praises; sing praises to our King, sing praises.

Psalm 47:6

MAY 7

Morning: I will sing to the LORD, for he has been good to me.

Psalm 13:6

Evening: "Because he loves me," says the LORD, "I will rescue him; I will protect him, for he acknowledges my name."

Psalm 91:14

MAY 8

Morning: Praise the LORD, O my soul. O LORD my God, you are very great; you are clothed with splendor and majesty.

Psalm 104:1

Evening: How can I repay the LORD for all his goodness to me?

Psalm 116:12

MAY 9

Morning: I will hasten and not delay to obey your commands.

Psalm 119:60

Evening: But God has surely listened and heard my voice in prayer.

Psalm 66:19

MAY 10

Morning: Guide me in your truth and teach me, for you are God my Savior, and my hope is in you all day long.

Psalm 25:5

Evening: Be not far from me, O God; come quickly, O my God, to help me.

Psalm 71:12

MAY 11

Morning: Come, let us bow down in worship, let us kneel before the LORD our Maker.

Psalm 95:6

Evening: O LORD, by your hand save me from such men, from men of this world whose reward is in this life.

Psalm 17:14

MAY 12

Morning: Accept, O LORD, the willing praise of my mouth, and teach me your laws.

Psalm 119:108

Evening: I said to the LORD, "You are my LORD; apart from you I have no good thing."

Psalm 16:2

MAY 13

Morning: The LORD reigns, let the earth be glad; let the distant shores rejoice.

Psalm 97:1

Evening: Let not those gloat over me who are my enemies without cause; let not those who hate me without reason maliciously wink the eye.

Psalm 35:19

MAY 14

Morning: The LORD is God, and he has made his light shine upon us.

Psalm 118:27

Evening: Your word, O LORD, is eternal; it stands firm in the heavens.

Psalm 119:89

MAY 15

Morning: Blessed are those whose strength is in you, who have set their hearts on pilgrimage.

Psalm 84:5

Evening: The LORD is compassionate and gracious, slow to anger, abounding in love.

Psalm 103:8

MAY 16

Morning: Be exalted, O God, above the heavens, and let your glory be over all the earth.

Psalm 108:5

Evening: Do good, O LORD, to those who are good, to those who are upright in heart.

Psalm 125:4

MAY 17

Morning: In the night I remember your name, O LORD, and I will keep your law.

Psalm 119:55

Evening: I will praise you as long as I live, and in your name I will lift up my hands.

Psalm 62:4

MAY 18

Morning: Wait for the LORD; be strong and take heart and wait for the LORD.

Psalm 27:14

Evening: Though I constantly take my life in my hands, I will not forget your law.

Psalm 119:109

MAY 19

Morning: How awesome is the LORD Most High, the great King over all the earth!

Psalm 47:2

Evening: Trust in him at all times, O people; pour out your hearts to him, for God is our refuge. Selah

Psalm 62:8

MAY 20

Morning: I will sing to the LORD all my life; I will sing praise to my God as long as I live.

Psalm 104:33

Evening: I will give you thanks, for you answered me; you have become my salvation.

Psalm 118:21

MAY 21

Morning: I will never forget your precepts, for by them you have preserved my life.

Psalm 119:93

Evening: Love and faithfulness meet together; righteousness and peace kiss each other.

Psalm 85:10

MAY 22

Morning: Hear my prayer, O LORD; listen to my cry for mercy.

Psalm 86:6

Evening: The LORD is with me; I will not be afraid. What can man do to me?

Psalm 118:6

MAY 23

Morning: Sing to the LORD a new song; sing to the LORD, all the earth.

Psalm 96:1

Evening: For the word of the LORD is right and true; he is faithful in all he does.

Psalm 33:4

MAY 24

Morning: All the earth bows down to you; they sing praise to you, they sing praise to your name. Selah

Psalm 66:4

Evening: God is our refuge and strength, an ever-present help in trouble.

Psalm 46:1

MAY 25

Morning: Because you are my help, I sing in the shadow of your wings.

Psalm 62:7

Evening: Blessed are those who dwell in your house; they are ever praising you. Selah

Psalm 84:4

MAY 26

Morning: Let us come before him with thanksgiving and extol him with music and song.

Psalm 95:2

Evening: Help me, O LORD my God; save me in accordance with your love.

Psalm 109:26

MAY 27

Morning: Bring joy to your servant, for to you, O LORD, I lift up my soul.

Psalm 86:4

Evening: Restore to me the joy of your salvation and grant me a willing spirit, to sustain me.

Psalm 51:12

MAY 28

Morning: This is the day the LORD has made; let us rejoice and be glad in it.

Psalm 118:24

Evening: In God, whose word I praise, in God I trust; I will not be afraid. What can mortal man do to me?

Psalm 56:4

MAY 29

Morning: Sing to the LORD, praise his name; proclaim his salvation day after day.

Psalm 96:2

Evening: But you remain the same, and your years will never end.

Psalm 102:27

MAY 30

Morning: For he stands at the right hand of the needy one, to save his life from those who condemn him.

Psalm 109:31

Evening: The law of the LORD is perfect, reviving the soul. The statutes of the LORD are trustworthy, making wise the simple.

Psalm 19:7

MAY 31

Morning: Hear my cry for mercy as I call to you for help, as I lift up my hands toward your Most Holy Place.

Psalm 28:2

Evening: I will praise you, O LORD, with all my heart; I will tell of all your wonders.

Psalm 9:1

JUNE 1

Morning: To him who led his people through the desert, His love endures forever.

Psalm 136:16

Evening: For the LORD watches over the way of the righteous, but the way of the wicked will perish.

Psalm 1:6

JUNE 2

Morning: Be still before the LORD and wait patiently for him; do not fret when men succeed in their ways, when they carry out their wicked schemes.

Psalm 37:7

Evening: The sacrifices of God are a broken spirit; a broken and contrite heart, O God, you will not despise.

Psalm 51:17

JUNE 3

Morning: Praise be to the LORD, to God our Savior, who daily bears our burdens. Selah

Psalm 68:19

Evening: May my meditation be pleasing to him, as I rejoice in the LORD.

Psalm 104:34

JUNE 4

Morning: But I cry to you for help, O LORD; in the morning my prayer comes before you.

Psalm 88:13

Evening: Who can proclaim the mighty acts of the LORD or fully declare his praise?

Psalm 106:2

JUNE 5

Morning: The fear of the LORD is the beginning of wisdom; all who follow his precepts have good understanding. To him belongs eternal praise.

Psalm 111:10

Evening: Man is like a breath; his days are like a fleeting shadow.

Psalm 144:4

JUNE 6

Morning: Be at rest once more, O my soul, for the LORD has been good to you.

Psalm 116:7

Evening: With long life will I satisfy him and show him my salvation.

Psalm 91:16

JUNE 7

Morning: Let them praise the name of the LORD, for he commanded and they were created.

Psalm 148:5

Evening: I seek you with all my heart; do not let me stray from your commands.

Psalm 119:10

JUNE 8

Morning: Shout for joy to the LORD, all the earth, burst into jubilant song with music.

Psalm 98:4

Evening: May my prayer come before you; turn your ear to my cry.

Psalm 88:2

JUNE 9

Morning: Praise our God, O peoples, let the sound of his praise be heard.

Psalm 66:8

Evening: For your love is ever before me, and I walk continually in your truth.

Psalm 26:3

JUNE 10

Morning: Teach me knowledge and good judgment, for I believe in your commands.

Psalm 119:66

Evening: I desire to do your will, O my God; your law is within my heart.

Psalm 40:8

JUNE 11

Morning: One thing God has spoken, two things have I heard: that you, O God, are strong, and that you, O LORD, are loving.

Psalm 62:11-12

Evening: How many are your works, O LORD! In wisdom you made them all; the earth is full of your creatures.

Psalm 104:24

JUNE 12

Morning: O LORD, the God who saves me, day and night I cry out before you.

Psalm 88:1

Evening: Glory in his holy name; let the hearts of those who seek the LORD rejoice.

Psalm 105:3

JUNE 13

Morning: I run in the path of your commands, for you have set my heart free.

Psalm 119:32

Evening: Yet I am poor and needy; come quickly to me, O God. You are my help and my deliverer; O LORD, do not delay.

Psalm 70:5

JUNE 14

Morning: Because he turned his ear to me, I will call on him as long as I live.

Psalm 116:2

Evening: May you be blessed by the LORD, the Maker of heaven and earth.

Psalm 116:15

JUNE 15

Morning: Give thanks to the LORD, call on his name; make known among the nations what he has done.

Psalm 105:1

Evening: I will remember the deeds of the LORD; yes, I will remember your miracles of long ago.

Psalm 77:11

JUNE 16

Morning: I will sing of the LORD's great love forever; with my mouth I will make your faithfulness known through all generations.

Psalm 89:1

Evening: For great is the LORD and most worthy of praise; he is to be feared above all gods.

Psalm 96:4

JUNE 17

Morning: He will bless those who fear the LORD—small and great alike.

Psalm 116:13

Evening: Ascribe to the LORD, O mighty ones, ascribe to the LORD glory and strength.

Psalm 29:1

JUNE 18

Morning: The LORD watches over the alien and sustains the fatherless and the widow, but he frustrates the ways of the wicked.

Psalm 146:9

Evening: You are forgiving and good, O LORD, abounding in love to all who call to you.

Psalm 86:5

JUNE 19

Morning: But the LORD has become my fortress, and my God the rock in whom I take refuge.

Psalm 94:22

Evening: O LORD, save us; O LORD, grant us success.

Psalm 118:25

JUNE 20

Morning: But from everlasting to everlasting the LORD's love is with those who fear him, and his righteousness with their children's children.

Psalm 103:17

Evening: Praise God in the great congregation; praise the LORD in the assembly of Israel.

Psalm 68:26

JUNE 21

Morning: Your statutes are my delight; they are my counselors.

Psalm 119:24

Evening: I lift up my eyes to you, to you whose throne is in heaven.

Psalm 123:1

JUNE 22

Morning: Let them know that you, whose name is the LORD—that you alone are the Most High over all the earth.

Psalm 83:18

Evening: For God is the King of all the earth; sing to him a psalm of praise.

Psalm 47:7

JUNE 23

Morning: For great is your love toward me; you have delivered me from the depths of the grave.

Psalm 86:13

Evening: We wait in hope for the LORD; he is our help and our shield.

Psalm 33:20

JUNE 24

Morning: But I will sing of your strength, in the morning I will sing of your love; for you are my fortress, my refuge in times of trouble.

Psalm 59:16

Evening: I will declare that your love stands firm forever, that you established your faithfulness in heaven itself.

Psalm 89:2

JUNE 25

Morning: The LORD will fulfill his purpose for me; your love, O LORD, endures forever—do not abandon the works of your hands.

Psalm 138:8

Evening: Within your temple, O God, we meditate on your unfailing love.

Psalm 48:9

JUNE 26

Morning: I will praise you with an upright heart as I learn your righteous laws.

Psalm 119:7

Evening: I call on the L ORD in my distress, and he answers me.

Psalm 120:1

JUNE 27

Morning: Sing to him, sing praise to him; tell of all his wonderful acts.

Psalm 105:2

Evening: Do not fret because of evil men or be envious of those who do wrong.

Psalm 37:1

JUNE 28

Morning: He provides food for those who fear him; he remembers his covenant forever.

Psalm 111:5

Evening: Answer me, O L ORD, out of the goodness of your love; in your great mercy turn to me.

Psalm 69:16

JUNE 29

Morning: Your statutes stand firm; holiness adorns your house for endless days, O LORD.

Psalm 93:5

Evening: My mouth will tell of your righteousness, of your salvation all day long, though I know not its measure.

Psalm 71:15

JUNE 30

Morning: With God we will gain the victory, and he will trample down our enemies.

Psalm 108:13

Evening: Have mercy on me, O God, have mercy on me, for in you my soul takes refuge. I will take refuge in the shadow of your wings until the disaster has passed.

Psalm 57:1

JULY 1

Morning: Be exalted, O LORD, in your strength; we will sing and praise your might.

Psalm 21:13

Evening: I will praise you forever for what you have done; in your name I will hope, for your name is good.

Psalm 52:9

JULY 2

Morning: May the glory of the LORD endure forever; may the LORD rejoice in his works.

Psalm 104:31

Evening: Oh, that my ways were steadfast in obeying your decrees!

Psalm 119:5

JULY 3

Morning: He put a new song in my mouth, a hymn of praise to our God. Many will see and fear and put their trust in the LORD.

Psalm 40:3

Evening: He will rescue them from oppression and violence, for precious is their blood in his sight.

Psalm 72:14

JULY 4

Morning: O LORD, the king rejoices in your strength. How great is his joy in the victories you give!

Psalm 21:1

Evening: I will extol the LORD at all times; his praise will always be on my lips.

Psalm 34:1

JULY 5

Morning: Search me, O God, and know my heart; test me and know my anxious thoughts.

Psalm 139:23

Evening: I will obey your decrees; do not utterly forsake me.

Psalm 119:8

JULY 6

Morning: Turn my eyes away from worthless things; preserve my life according to your word.

Psalm 119:37

Evening: With your hand you drove out the nations and planted our fathers; you crushed the peoples and made our fathers flourish.

Psalm 44:2

JULY 7

Morning: But you, O God, do see trouble and grief; you consider it to take it in hand. The victim commits himself to you; you are the helper of the fatherless.

Psalm 10:14

Evening: We have heard with our ears, O God; our fathers have told us what you did in their days, in days long ago.

Psalm 44:1

JULY 8

Morning: As we have heard, so have we seen in the city of the LORD Almighty, in the city of our God: God makes her secure forever. Selah

Psalm 48:8

Evening: But you, O LORD, sit enthroned forever; your renown endures through all generations.

Psalm 102:12

JULY 9

Morning: But you, O Sovereign LORD, deal well with me for your name's sake; out of the goodness of your love, deliver me.

Psalm 109:21

Evening: Help us, O God our Savior, for the glory of your name; deliver us and forgive our sins for your name's sake.

Psalm 79:9

JULY 10

Morning: Proclaim the power of God, whose majesty is over Israel, whose power is in the skies.

Psalm 68:34

Evening: But you, O LORD, are exalted forever.

Psalm 92:8

JULY 11

Morning: The arrogant cannot stand in your presence; you hate all who do wrong.

Psalm 5:5

Evening: Though he stumble, he will not fall, for the LORD upholds him with his hand.

Psalm 37:24

JULY 12

Morning: Whoever slanders his neighbor in secret, him will I put to silence; whoever has haughty eyes and a proud heart, him will I not endure.

Psalm 101:5

Evening: I have been blameless before him and have kept myself from sin.

Psalm 18:23

JULY 13

Morning: To him who alone does great wonders, His love endures forever.

Psalm 136:4

Evening: Man is a mere phantom as he goes to and fro: He bustles about, but only in vain; he heaps up wealth, not knowing who will get it.

Psalm 39:6

JULY 14

Morning: Mightier than the thunder of the great waters, mightier than the breakers of the sea—the LORD on high is mighty.

Psalm 93:4

Evening: Glorify the LORD with me; let us exalt his name together.

Psalm 34:3

JULY 15

Morning: Those who know your name will trust in you, for you, LORD, have never forsaken those who seek you.

Psalm 9:10

Evening: But you, O LORD, are a compassionate and gracious God, slow to anger, abounding in love and faithfulness.

Psalm 86:15

JULY 16

Morning: O God, whom I praise, do not remain silent.

Psalm 109

Evening: The LORD protects the simplehear when I was in great need, he saved me.

Ps

JULY 17

Morning: Teach me, O LORD, to follow your decrees; then I will keep them to the end.

Psalm 119:33

Evening: For the sake of your name, O LORD, forgive my iniquity, though it is great.

Psalm 25:11

JULY 18

Morning: The LORD is my rock, my fortress and my deliverer; my God is my rock, in whom I take refuge. He is my shield and the horn of my salvation, my stronghold.

Psalm 18:2

Evening: How priceless is your unfailing love! Both high and low among men find refuge in the shadow of your wings.

Psalm 36:7

JULY 19

Morning: Like your name, O God, your praise reaches to the ends of the earth; your right hand is filled with righteousness.

Psalm 48:10

Evening: Remember the wonders he has done, his miracles, and the judgments he pronounced.

Psalm 105:5

JULY 26

Morning: He is my loving God and my fortress, my stronghold and my deliverer, my shield, in whom I take refuge, who subdues peoples under me.

Psalm 144:2

Evening: Let those who fear the LORD say: "His love endures forever."

Psalm 118:4

JULY 27

Morning: For you make me glad by your deeds, O LORD; I sing for joy at the works of your hands.

Psalm 92:4

Evening: He has preserved our lives and kept our feet from slipping.

Psalm 66:9

JULY 28

Morning: For the LORD will vindicate his people and have compassion on his servants.

Psalm 135:14

Evening: I call to the LORD, who is worthy of praise, and I am saved from my enemies.

Psalm 18:3

JULY 29

Morning: Praise be to you, O LORD; teach me your decrees.

Psalm 119:12

Evening: Guard my life and rescue me; for I take refuge in you. let me not be put to shame.

Psalm 25:20

JULY 30

Morning: Save me, O LORD, from lying lips and from deceitful tongues.

Psalm 120:2

Evening: He has shown his people the power of his works, giving them the lands of other nations.

Psalm 111:6

JULY 31

Morning: Let the LORD judge the peoples. Judge me, O LORD, according to my righteousness, according to my integrity, O Most High.

Psalm 7:8

Evening: And the heavens proclaim his righteousness, for God himself is judge. Selah

Psalm 50:6

AUGUST 1

Morning: Serve the LORD with fear and rejoice with trembling.

Psalm 2:11

Evening: Take heed, you senseless ones among the people; you fools, when will you become wise?

Psalm 94:8

AUGUST 2

Morning: Even from birth the wicked go astray; from the womb they are wayward and speak lies.

Psalm 58:3

Evening: The LORD gives strength to his people; the LORD blesses his people with peace.

Psalm 29:11

AUGUST 3

Morning: From the lips of children and infants you have ordained praise because of your enemies, to silence the foe and the avenger.

Psalm 8:2

Evening: Turn to me and be gracious to me, for I am lonely and afflicted.

Psalm 25:16

AUGUST 4

Morning: He will take pity on the weak and the needy and save the needy from death.

Psalm 72:13

Evening: He will have no fear of bad news; his heart is steadfast, trusting in the LORD.

Psalm 112:7

AUGUST 5

Morning: They have greatly oppressed me from my youth, but they have not gained the victory over me.

Psalm 129:2

Evening: Let the wicked fall into their own nets, while I pass by in safety.

Psalm 141:10

AUGUST 6

Morning: The LORD is with me; he is my helper. I will look in triumph on my enemies.

Psalm 118:7

Evening: Sing to God, O kingdoms of the earth, sing praise to the LORD.

Psalm 68:32

AUGUST 7

Morning: Tremble, O earth, at the presence of the LORD, at the presence of the God of Jacob.

Psalm 114:7

Evening: The LORD is a refuge for the oppressed, a stronghold in times of trouble.

Psalm 9:9

AUGUST 8

Morning: Spread your protection over them, that those who love your name may rejoice in you.

Psalm 5:1

Evening: The LORD is the strength of his people, a fortress of salvation for his anointed one.

Psalm 28:8

AUGUST 9

Morning: He will not let your foot slip—he who watches over you will not slumber.

Psalm 121:3

Evening: I have not departed from your laws, for you yourself have taught me.

Psalm 119:102

AUGUST 10

Morning: Declare his glory among the nations, his marvelous deeds among all peoples.

Psalm 96:3

Evening: Let all the earth fear the LORD; let all the people of the world revere him.

Psalm 33:8

AUGUST 11

Morning: For the LORD loves the just and will not forsake his faithful ones.

Psalm 37:28

Evening: My comfort in my suffering is this: Your promise preserves my life.

Psalm 119:50

AUGUST 12

Morning: Good will come to him who is generous and lends freely, who conducts his affairs with justice.

Psalm 112:5

Evening: Even the sparrow has found a home, and the swallow a nest for herself, where she may have her young—a place near your altar, O LORD Almighty, my King and my God.

Psalm 84:3

AUGUST 13

Morning: Summon your power, O God; show us your strength, O God, as you have done before.

Psalm 68:28

Evening: He will endure as long as the sun, as long as the moon, through all generations.

Psalm 72:5

AUGUST 14

Morning: But the meek will inherit the land and enjoy great peace.

Psalm 37:11

Evening: Your throne was established long ago; you are from all eternity.

Psalm 93:2

AUGUST 15

Morning: Then will I go to the altar of God, to God, my joy and my delight. I will praise you with the harp, O God, my God.

Psalm 43:4

Evening: I will be careful to lead a blameless life—when will you come to me? I will walk in my house with blameless heart.

Psalm 101:2

AUGUST 16

Morning: He sent forth his word and healed them; he rescued them from the grave.

Psalm 107:20

Evening: Save us, O LORD our God, and gather us from the nations, that we may give thanks to your holy name and glory in your praise.

Psalm 106:47

AUGUST 17

Morning: The righteous will inherit the land and dwell in it forever.

Psalm 37:29

Evening: A thousand may fall at your side, ten thousand at your right hand, but it will not come near you.

Psalm 91:7

AUGUST 18

Morning: O righteous God, who searches minds and hearts, bring to an end the violence of the wicked and make the righteous secure.

Psalm 7:9

Evening: Righteousness and justice are the foundation of your throne; love and faithfulness go before you.

Psalm 89:14

AUGUST 19

Morning: I will praise the LORD all my life; I will sing praise to my God as long as I live.

Psalm 146:2

Evening: Praise the LORD with the harp; make music to him on the ten-stringed lyre.

Psalm 33:2

AUGUST 20

Morning: Restore us again, O God our Savior, and put away your displeasure toward us.

Psalm 85:4

Evening: May his name endure forever; may it continue as long as the sun. All nations will be blessed through him, and they will call him blessed.

Psalm 72:17

AUGUST 21

Morning: Praise the LORD. Praise, O servants of the LORD, praise the name of the LORD.

Psalm 113:1

Evening: You open your hand and satisfy the desires of every living thing.

Psalm 145:16

AUGUST 22

Morning: I will exalt you, my God the King; I will praise your name for ever and ever.

Psalm 145:1

Evening: Blessed is the man you discipline, O LORD, the man you teach from your law.

Psalm 94:12

AUGUST 23

Morning: From birth I was cast upon you; from my mother's womb you have been my God.

Psalm 22:10

Evening: Who forgives all your sins and heals all your diseases, ... who satisfies your desires with good things so that your youth is renewed like the eagle's.

Psalm 103:3,5

AUGUST 24

Morning: Praise the LORD. How good it is to sing praises to our God, how pleasant and fitting to praise him!

Psalm 147:1

Evening: Remember me, O LORD, when you show favor to your people, come to my aid when you save them.

Psalm 106:4

AUGUST 25

Morning: I will listen to what God the LORD will say; he promises peace to his people, his saints—but let them not return to folly.

Psalm 85:8

Evening: Before the mountains were born or you brought forth the earth and the world, from everlasting to everlasting you are God.

Psalm 90:2

AUGUST 26

Morning: Know that the LORD has set apart the godly for himself; the LORD will hear when I call to him.

Psalm 4:3

Evening: As far as the east is from the west, so far has he removed our transgressions from us.

Psalm 103:12

AUGUST 27

Morning: Let your compassion come to me that I may live, for your law is my delight.

Psalm 119:77

Evening: He will cover you with his feathers, and under his wings you will find refuge; his faithfulness will be your shield and rampart.

Psalm 91:4

AUGUST 28

Morning: But the plans of the LORD stand firm forever, the purposes of his heart through all generations.

Psalm 33:11

Evening: In your unfailing love, silence my enemies; destroy all my foes, for I am your servant.

Psalm 143:12

AUGUST 29

Morning: May all the kings of the earth praise you, O LORD, when they hear the words of your mouth.

Psalm 138:4

Evening: But I am like an olive tree flourishing in the house of God; I trust in God's unfailing love for ever and ever.

Psalm 52:8

AUGUST 30

Morning: In the council of the holy ones God is greatly feared; he is more awesome than all who surround him.

Psalm 89:7

Evening: He raises the poor from the dust and lifts the needy from the ash heap.

Psalm 113:7

AUGUST 31

Morning: Pray for the peace of Jerusalem: "May those who love you be secure."

Psalm 122:6

Evening: Blessed is he who has regard for the weak; the LORD delivers him in times of trouble.

Psalm 41:1

SEPTEMBER 1

Morning: Direct me in the path of your commands, for there I find delight.

Psalm 119:35

Evening: Light is shed upon the righteous and joy on the upright in heart.

Psalm 97:11

SEPTEMBER 2

Morning: Teach me to do your will, for you are my God; may your good Spirit lead me on level ground.

Psalm 143:10

Evening: Be merciful to me, LORD, for I am faint; O LORD, heal me, for my bones are in agony.

Psalm 6:2

SEPTEMBER 3

Morning: He provided redemption for his people; he ordained his covenant forever—holy and awesome is his name.

Psalm 111:9

Evening: LORD, do not rebuke me in your anger or discipline me in your wrath.

Psalm 38:1

SEPTEMBER 4

Morning: All the nations you have made will come and worship before you, O LORD; they will bring glory to your name.

Psalm 86:9

Evening: May God arise, may his enemies be scattered; may his foes flee before him.

Psalm 68:1

SEPTEMBER 5

Morning: Those who trust in the LORD are like Mount Zion, which cannot be shaken but endures forever.

Psalm 125:1

Evening: If I go up to the heavens, you are there; if I make my bed in the depths, you are there.

Psalm 139:8

SEPTEMBER 6

Morning: O LORD, hear my prayer, listen to my cry for mercy; in your faithfulness and righteousness come to my relief.

Psalm 143:1

Evening: God looks down from heaven on the sons of men to see if there are any who understand, any who seek God.

Psalm 53:2

SEPTEMBER 7

Morning: For I delight in your commands because I love them.

Psalm 119:47

Evening: Those living far away fear your wonders; where morning dawns and evening fades you call forth songs of joy.

Psalm 65:8

SEPTEMBER 8

Morning: Blessed are all who fear the LORD, who walk in his ways.

Psalm 128:1

Evening: The LORD has made his salvation known and revealed his righteousness to the nations.

Psalm 98:2

SEPTEMBER 9

Morning: Keep me safe, O God, for in you I take refuge.

Psalm 16:1

Evening: Whom have I in heaven but you? And earth has nothing I desire besides you.

Psalm 73:25

SEPTEMBER 10

Morning: My soul thirsts for God, for the living God. When can I go and meet with God?

Psalm 42:2

Evening: I love you, O LORD, my strength.

Psalm 18:1

SEPTEMBER 11

Morning: Praise the LORD. Praise the name of the LORD; praise him, you servants of the LORD.

Psalm 135:1

Evening: The heavens declare the glory of God; the skies proclaim the work of his hands.

Psalm 19:1

SEPTEMBER 12

Morning: Out of the depths I cry to you, O LORD.

Psalm 130:1

Evening: To all perfection I see a limit; but your commands are boundless.

Psalm 119:96

SEPTEMBER 13

Morning: By day the LORD directs his love, at night his song is with me—a prayer to the God of my life.

Psalm 42:8

Evening: In your anger do not sin; when you are on your beds, search your hearts and be silent. Selah

Psalm 4:4

SEPTEMBER 14

Morning: The LORD looks down from heaven on the sons of men to see if there are any who understand, any who seek God.

Psalm 14:2

Evening: For you have been my refuge, a strong tower against the foe.

Psalm 61:3

SEPTEMBER 15

Morning: The LORD's right hand is lifted high; the LORD's right hand has done mighty things!
Psalm 118:16

Evening: Righteousness goes before him and prepares the way for his steps.
Psalm 85:13

SEPTEMBER 16

Morning: The mouth of the righteous man utters wisdom, and his tongue speaks what is just.
Psalm 37:30

Evening: He has caused his wonders to be remembered; the LORD is gracious and compassionate.
Psalm 111:4

SEPTEMBER 17

Morning: Do not be overawed when a man grows rich, when the splendor of his house increases.
Psalm 49:16

Evening: From the rising of the sun to the place where it sets, the name of the LORD is to be praised.
Psalm 113:3

SEPTEMBER 18

Morning: Give me understanding, and I will keep your law and obey it with all my heart.
Psalm 119:34

Evening: For you have been my hope, O Sovereign LORD, my confidence since my youth.
Psalm 71:5

SEPTEMBER 19

Morning: Lift up your hands in the sanctuary and praise the LORD.
Psalm 134:2

Evening: But now, LORD, what do I look for? My hope is in you.
Psalm 39:7

SEPTEMBER 20

Morning: Your commands make me wiser than my enemies, for they are ever with me.
Psalm 119:98

Evening: O Israel, put your hope in the LORD, for with the LORD is unfailing love and with him is full redemption.
Psalm 130:7

SEPTEMBER 21

Morning: Praise him for his acts of power; praise him for his surpassing greatness.

Psalm 150:2

Evening: Those the LORD blesses will inherit the land, but those he curses will be cut off.

Psalm 37:22

SEPTEMBER 22

Morning: I have considered my ways and have turned my steps to your statutes.

Psalm 119:59

Evening: May the words of my mouth and the meditation of my heart be pleasing in your sight, O LORD, my Rock and my Redeemer.

Psalm 19:14

SEPTEMBER 23

Morning: When I called, you answered me; you made me bold and stouthearted.

Psalm 138:3

Evening: You guide me with your counsel, and afterward you will take me into glory.

Psalm 73:24

SEPTEMBER 24

Morning: The LORD watches over you—the LORD is your shade at your right hand.

Psalm 121:5

Evening: Surely his salvation is near those who fear him, that his glory may dwell in our land.

Psalm 85:9

SEPTEMBER 25

Morning: For you have heard my vows, O God; you have given me the heritage of those who fear your name.

Psalm 61:5

Evening: I know that the LORD secures justice for the poor and upholds the cause of the needy.

Psalm 140:12

SEPTEMBER 26

Morning: They are always generous and lend freely; their children will be blessed.

Psalm 37:26

Evening: He restores my soul. He guides me in paths of righteousness.

Psalm 23:3

SEPTEMBER 27

Morning: The LORD is gracious and compassionate, slow to anger and rich in love.

Psalm 145:8

Evening: The LORD will sustain him on his sickbed and restore him from his bed of illness.

Psalm 41:3

SEPTEMBER 28

Morning: For the LORD is righteous, he loves justice; upright men will see his face.

Psalm 11:7

Evening: My eyes will be on the faithful in the land, that they may dwell with me; he whose walk is blameless will minister to me.

Psalm 101:6

SEPTEMBER 29

Morning: Praise the LORD, for the LORD is good; sing praise to his name, for that is pleasant.

Psalm 135:3

Evening: I have chosen the way of truth; I have set my heart on your laws.

Psalm 119:30

SEPTEMBER 30

Morning: I will praise you, O LORD, with all my heart; before the "gods" I will sing your praise.

Psalm 138:1

Evening: His children will be mighty in the land; the generation of the upright will be blessed.

Psalm 112:2

OCTOBER 1

Morning: Let them give thanks to the LORD for his unfailing love and his wonderful deeds for men.

Psalm 107:15

Evening: In you I trust, O my God. Do not let me be put to shame, nor let my enemies triumph over me.

Psalm 25:2

OCTOBER 2

Morning: I will sing a new song to you, O God; on the ten-stringed lyre I will make music to you.

Psalm 144:9

Evening: Contend, O LORD, with those who contend with me; fight against those who fight against me.

Psalm 35:1

OCTOBER 3

Morning: My soul will be satisfied as with the richest of foods; with singing lips my mouth will praise you.

Psalm 62:5

Evening: Praise the LORD, all you servants of the LORD who minister by night in the house of the LORD.

Psalm 134:1

OCTOBER 4

Morning: Blessed is he whose transgressions are forgiven, whose sins are covered.

Psalm 32:1

Evening: Turn to me and have mercy on me; grant your strength to your servant and save the son of your maidservant.

Psalm 86:16

OCTOBER 5

Morning: How can a young man keep his way pure? By living according to your word.

Psalm 119:9

Evening: He will call upon me, and I will answer him; I will be with him in trouble, I will deliver him and honor him.

Psalm 91:15

OCTOBER 6

Morning: For the LORD will not reject his people; he will never forsake his inheritance.

Psalm 94:14

Evening: For he satisfies the thirsty and fills the hungry with good things.

Psalm 107:9

OCTOBER 7

Morning: Praise the LORD. Praise the LORD from the heavens, praise him in the heights above.

Psalm 148:1

Evening: Let me understand the teaching of your precepts; then I will meditate on your wonders.

Psalm 119:27

OCTOBER 8

Morning: Your name, O LORD, endures forever, your renown, O LORD, through all generations.

Psalm 135:13

Evening: LORD, you have assigned me my portion and my cup; you have made my lot secure.

Psalm 16:5

OCTOBER 9

Morning: I call on you, O God, for you will answer me; give ear to me and hear my prayer.
Psalm 17:6

Evening: Therefore we will not fear, though the earth give way and the mountains fall into the heart of the sea.
Psalm 46:2

OCTOBER 10

Morning: They will speak of the glorious splendor of your majesty, and I will meditate on your wonderful works.
Psalm 145:5

Evening: For you, O God, tested us; you refined us like silver.
Psalm 66:10

OCTOBER 11

Morning: Your decrees are the theme of my song wherever I lodge.
Psalm 119:54

Evening: He chose our inheritance for us, the pride of Jacob, whom he loved. Selah
Psalm 47:4

OCTOBER 12

Morning: O LORD, hear my voice. Let your ears be attentive to my cry for mercy.

Psalm 130:2

Evening: Do good to your servant, and I will live; I will obey your word.

Psalm 119:17

OCTOBER 13

Morning: I know that the LORD is great, that our LORD is greater than all gods.

Psalm 135:5

Evening: The LORD works righteousness and justice for all the oppressed.

Psalm 103:6

OCTOBER 14

Morning: He will make your righteousness shine like the dawn, the justice of your cause like the noonday sun.

Psalm 37:6

Evening: He reached down from on high and took hold of me; he drew me out of deep waters.

Psalm 18:16

OCTOBER 15

Morning: Thus is the man blessed who fears the LORD.

Psalm 128:4

Evening: You love righteousness and hate wickedness; therefore God, your God, has set you above your companions by anointing you with the oil of joy.

Psalm 45:7

OCTOBER 16

Morning: Come, my children, listen to me; I will teach you the fear of the LORD.

Psalm 34:11

Evening: The LORD watches over all who love him, but all the wicked he will destroy.

Psalm 145:20

OCTOBER 17

Morning: You answer us with awesome deeds of righteousness, O God our Savior, the hope of all the ends of the earth and of the farthest seas.

Psalm 65:5

Evening: This has been my practice: I obey your precepts.

Psalm 119:56

OCTOBER 18

Morning: The LORD is near to all who call on him, to all who call on him in truth.

Psalm 145:18

Evening: You forgave the iniquity of your people and covered all their sins. Selah

Psalm 85:2

OCTOBER 19

Morning: We have sinned, even as our fathers did; we have done wrong and acted wickedly.

Psalm 106:6

Evening: But for those who fear you, you have raised a banner to be unfurled against the bow. Selah

Psalm 60:4

OCTOBER 20

Morning: I long to dwell in your tent forever and take refuge in the shelter of your wings. Selah

Psalm 61:4

Evening: The children of your servants will live in your presence; their descendants will be established before you.

Psalm 102:28

OCTOBER 21

Morning: I lift up my hands to your commands, which I love, and I meditate on your decrees.

Psalm 119:48

Evening: Your righteousness is like the mighty mountains, your justice like the great deep. O LORD, you preserve both man and beast.

Psalm 36:6

OCTOBER 22

Morning: The LORD is my shepherd, I shall not be in want.

Psalm 23:1

Evening: The LORD delights in those who fear him, who put their hope in his unfailing love.

Psalm 147:11

OCTOBER 23

Morning: Praise be to the LORD, for he has heard my cry for mercy.

Psalm 28:6

Evening: You are the most excellent of men and your lips have been anointed with grace, since God has blessed you forever.

Psalm 45:2

OCTOBER 24

Morning: Your hands made me and formed me; give me understanding to learn your commands.

Psalm 119:73

Evening: Wait for the LORD and keep his way. He will exalt you to inherit the land; when the wicked are cut off, you will see it.

Psalm 37:34

OCTOBER 25

Morning: The angel of the LORD encamps around those who fear him, and he delivers them.

Psalm 34:7

Evening: The streams of God are filled with water to provide the people with grain, for so you have ordained it.

Psalm 65:9

OCTOBER 26

Morning: Praise him, all his angels, praise him, all his heavenly hosts.

Psalm 148:2

Evening: The earth is filled with your love, O LORD; teach me your decrees.

Psalm 119:64

OCTOBER 27

Morning: Surely the righteous will praise your name and the upright will live before you.

Psalm 140:13

Evening: Then they would put their trust in God and would not forget his deeds but would keep his commands.

Psalm 78:7

OCTOBER 28

Morning: Sing to him a new song; play skillfully, and shout for joy.

Psalm 33:3

Evening: Then will I ever sing praise to your name and fulfill my vows day after day.

Psalm 61:8

OCTOBER 29

Morning: Praise the LORD. Praise God in his sanctuary; praise him in his mighty heavens.

Psalm 150:1

Evening: Turn my heart toward your statutes and not toward selfish gain.

Psalm 119:36

OCTOBER 30

Morning: The righteous cry out, and the LORD hears them; he delivers them from all their troubles.

Psalm 34:17

Evening: For the LORD takes delight in his people; he crowns the humble with salvation.

Psalm 149:4

OCTOBER 31

Morning: You have shaken the land and torn it open; mend its fractures, for it is quaking.

Psalm 60:2

Evening: In my anguish I cried to the LORD, and he answered by setting me free.

Psalm 118:5

NOVEMBER 1

Morning: The LORD is exalted over all the nations, his glory above the heavens.

Psalm 113:4

Evening: For evil men will be cut off, but those who hope in the LORD will inherit the land.

Psalm 37:9

NOVEMBER 2

Morning: I have sought your face with all my heart; be gracious to me according to your promise.

Psalm 119:58

Evening: For this God is our God for ever and ever; he will be our guide even to the end.

Psalm 48:14

NOVEMBER 3

Morning: How precious to me are your thoughts, O God! How vast is the sum of them!

Psalm 139:17

Evening: From heaven the LORD looks down and sees all mankind.

Psalm 33:13

NOVEMBER 4

Morning: I cry to you, O LORD; I say, "You are my refuge, my portion in the land of the living."

Psalm 142:5

Evening: May he give you the desire of your heart and make all your plans succeed.

Psalm 20:4

NOVEMBER 5

Morning: Blessed is he who comes in the name of the LORD. From the house of the LORD we bless you.

Psalm 118:26

Evening: Every day I will praise you and extol your name for ever and ever.

Psalm 145:2

NOVEMBER 6

Morning: Your ways, O God, are holy. What god is so great as our God?

Psalm 77:13

Evening: I sought the LORD, and he answered me; he delivered me from all my fears.

Psalm 34:4

NOVEMBER 7

Morning: My help comes from the LORD, the Maker of heaven and earth.

Psalm 121:2

Evening: My soul is weary with sorrow; strengthen me according to your word.

Psalm 119:28

NOVEMBER 8

Morning: But as for me, it is good to be near God. I have made the Sovereign LORD my refuge; I will tell of all your deeds.

Psalm 73:28

Evening: All you have made will praise you, O LORD; your saints will extol you.

Psalm 145:10

NOVEMBER 9

Morning: May the LORD answer you when you are in distress; may the name of the God of Jacob protect you.

Psalm 20:1

Evening: The LORD upholds all those who fall and lifts up all who are bowed down.

Psalm 145:14

NOVEMBER 10

Morning: Keep me, O LORD, from the hands of the wicked; protect me from men of violence who plan to trip my feet.

Psalm 140:4

Evening: May those who fear you rejoice when they see me, for I have put my hope in your word.

Psalm 119:74

NOVEMBER 11

Morning: From birth I have relied on you; you brought me forth from my mother's womb. I will ever praise you.

Psalm 71:6

Evening: Let the name of the LORD be praised, both now and forevermore.

Psalm 113:2

NOVEMBER 12

Morning: I will not die but live, and will proclaim what the LORD has done.

Psalm 118:17

Evening: He rules forever by his power, his eyes watch the nations—let not the rebellious rise up against him. Selah

Psalm 66:7

NOVEMBER 13

Morning: The LORD is faithful to all his promises and loving toward all he has made.

Psalm 145:13

Evening: The LORD redeems his servants; no one will be condemned who takes refuge in him.

Psalm 34:22

NOVEMBER 14

Morning: Whoever of you loves life and desires to see many good days, keep your tongue from evil and your lips from speaking lies.

Psalm 34:12-13

Evening: Open my eyes that I may see wonderful things in your law.

Psalm 119:18

NOVEMBER 15

Morning: Praise him with the clash of cymbals, praise him with resounding cymbals.

Psalm 150:5

Evening: My mouth will speak words of wisdom; the utterance from my heart will give understanding.

Psalm 49:3

NOVEMBER 16

Morning: Our help is in the name of the LORD, the Maker of heaven and earth.

Psalm 124:8

Evening: A man who has riches without understanding is like the beasts that perish.

Psalm 49:12

NOVEMBER 17

Morning: The LORD is righteous in all his ways and loving toward all he has made.

Psalm 145:17

Evening: Deliver me, O my God, from the hand of the wicked, from the grasp of evil and cruel men.

Psalm 71:4

NOVEMBER 18

Morning: Preserve my life according to your love, and I will obey the statutes of your mouth.

Psalm 119:88

Evening: The fool says in his heart, "There is no God." They are corrupt, and their ways are vile; there is no one who does good.

Psalm 53:1

NOVEMBER 19

Morning: The LORD will keep you from all harm—he will watch over your life.

Psalm 121:7

Evening: Do not put your trust in princes, in mortal men, who cannot save.

Psalm 146:3

NOVEMBER 20

Morning: Praise him with the sounding of the trumpet, Praise the LORD.

Psalm 150:3

Evening: Let the heavens rejoice, let the earth be glad; let the sea resound, and all that is in it.

Psalm 96:11

NOVEMBER 21

Morning: Praise the LORD from the earth, you great sea creatures and all ocean depths.

Psalm 148:7

Evening: Better the little that the righteous have than the wealth of many wicked.

Psalm 37:16

NOVEMBER 22

Morning: I delight in your decrees; I will not neglect your word.

Psalm 119:16

Evening: Reach down your hand from on high; deliver me and rescue me from the mighty waters, from the hands of foreigners.

Psalm 144:7

NOVEMBER 23

Morning: You discern my going out and my lying down; you are familiar with all my ways.

Psalm 139:3

Evening: It was good for me to be afflicted so that I might learn your decrees.

Psalm 119:71

NOVEMBER 24

Morning: Those who sow in tears will reap with songs of joy.

Psalm 126:5

Evening: May the foot of the proud not come against me, nor the hand of the wicked drive me away.

Psalm 36:11

NOVEMBER 25

Morning: Sing to the LORD with thanksgiving; make music to our God on the harp.

Psalm 147:7

Evening: I am a friend to all who fear you, to all who follow your precepts.

Psalm 119:63

NOVEMBER 26

Morning: The voice of the LORD is over the waters; the God of glory thunders, the LORD thunders over the mighty waters.

Psalm 29:3

Evening: Judgment will again be founded on righteousness, and all the upright in heart will follow it.

Psalm 94:15

NOVEMBER 27

Morning: They will sing before the LORD, for he comes, he comes to judge the earth. He will judge the world in righteousness and the peoples in his truth.

Psalm 96:13

Evening: Men of perverse heart shall be far from me; I will have nothing to do with evil.

Psalm 101:4

NOVEMBER 28

Morning: I will walk about in freedom, for I have sought out your precepts.

Psalm 119:45

Evening: The LORD knows the thoughts of man; he knows that they are futile.

Psalm 94:11

NOVEMBER 29

Morning: Those who look to him are radiant; their faces are never covered with shame.

Psalm 34:5

Evening: I will be glad and rejoice in your love, for you saw my affliction and knew the anguish of my soul.

Psalm 31:7

NOVEMBER 30

Morning: To the LORD I cry aloud, and he answers me from his holy hill. Selah

Psalm 3:4

Evening: I do not hide your righteousness in my heart; I speak of your faithfulness and salvation. I do not conceal your love and your truth from the great assembly.

Psalm 40:10

DECEMBER 1

Morning: He heals the brokenhearted and binds up their wounds.

Psalm 147:3

Evening: You have laid down precepts that are to be fully obeyed.

Psalm 119:4

DECEMBER 2

Morning: But the LORD is righteous; he has cut me free from the cords of the wicked.

Psalm 129:4

Evening: Into your hands I commit my spirit; redeem me, O LORD, the God of truth.

Psalm 31:5

DECEMBER 3

Morning: Let not my heart be drawn to what is evil, to take part in wicked deeds with men who are evildoers; let me not eat of their delicacies.

Psalm 141:4

Evening: Since you are my rock and my fortress, for the sake of your name lead and guide me.

Psalm 31:3

DECEMBER 4

Morning: May your unfailing love be my comfort, according to your promise to your servant.

Psalm 119:76

Evening: But let all who take refuge in you be glad; let them ever sing for joy.

Psalm 5:11

DECEMBER 5

Morning: See if there is any offensive way in me, and lead me in the way everlasting.

Psalm 139:24

Evening: For with you is the fountain of life; in your light we see light.

Psalm 36:9

DECEMBER 6

Morning: Rescue me from my enemies, O LORD, for I hide myself in you.

Psalm 143:9

Evening: Blessed are they whose ways are blameless, who walk according to the law of the LORD.

Psalm 119:1

DECEMBER 7

Morning: But I trust in your unfailing love; my heart rejoices in your salvation.

Psalm 13:5

Evening: Surely he will never be shaken; a righteous man will be remembered forever.

Psalm 112:6

DECEMBER 8

Morning: I rejoice in following your statutes as one rejoices in great riches.

Psalm 119:14

Evening: Let them know that it is your hand, that you, O LORD, have done it.

Psalm 109:27

DECEMBER 9

Morning: To you, O LORD, I called; to the LORD I cried for mercy.

Psalm 30:8

Evening: Give us aid against the enemy, for the help of man is worthless.

Psalm 60:11

DECEMBER 10

Morning: I wait for the LORD, my soul waits, and in his word I put my hope.

Psalm 130:5

Evening: Be my rock of refuge, to which I can always go; give the command to save me, for you are my rock and my fortress.

Psalm 71:3

DECEMBER 11

Morning: You are my God, and I will give you thanks; you are my God, and I will exalt you.

Psalm 118:28

Evening: The heavens praise your wonders, O LORD, your faithfulness too, in the assembly of the holy ones.

Psalm 89:5

DECEMBER 12

Morning: All your commands are trustworthy; help me, for men persecute me without cause.

Psalm 119:86

Evening: Praise him, you highest heavens and you waters above the skies.

Psalm 148:4

DECEMBER 13

Morning: How sweet are your words to my taste, sweeter than honey to my mouth!

Psalm 119:103

Evening: Restore us, O God; make your face shine upon us, that we may be saved.

Psalm 80:3

DECEMBER 14

Morning: I will give thanks to the LORD because of his righteousness and will sing praise to the name of the LORD Most High.

Psalm 7:17

Evening: My eyes are ever on the LORD, for only he will release my feet from the snare.

Psalm 25:15

DECEMBER 15

Morning: Good and upright is the LORD; therefore he instructs sinners in his ways.

Psalm 25:8

Evening: I gain understanding from your precepts; therefore I hate every wrong path.

Psalm 119:104

DECEMBER 16

Morning: Let the morning bring me word of your unfailing love, for I have put my trust in you. Show me the way I should go, for to you I lift up my soul.

Psalm 143:8

Evening: For your name's sake, O LORD, preserve my life; in your righteousness, bring me out of trouble.

Psalm 143:11

DECEMBER 17

Morning: My tongue will speak of your righteousness and of your praises all day long.

Psalm 35:28

Evening: But with you there is forgiveness; therefore you are feared.

Psalm 130:4

DECEMBER 18

Morning: Do not let the oppressed retreat in disgrace; may the poor and needy praise your name.

Psalm 74:21

Evening: Praise him, you highest heavens and you waters above the skies.

Psalm 148:4

DECEMBER 19

Morning: Remember not the sins of my youth and my rebellious ways; according to your love remember me, for you are good, O LORD.

Psalm 25:7

Evening: Then we your people, the sheep of your pasture, will praise you forever; from generation to generation we will recount your praise.

Psalm 79:13

DECEMBER 20

Morning: Some trust in chariots and some in horses, but we trust in the name of the LORD our God.

Psalm 20:7

Evening: O LORD, I say to you, "You are my God." Hear, O LORD, my cry for mercy.

Psalm 140:6

DECEMBER 21

Morning: If I rise on the wings of the dawn, if I settle on the far side of the sea, even there your and will guide me, your right hand will hold me fast.

Psalm 139:9-10

Evening: I have kept my feet from every evil path so that I might obey your word.

Psalm 119:101

DECEMBER 22

Morning: Great is our LORD and mighty in power; his understanding has no limit.

Psalm 147:5

Evening: You prepare a table before me in the presence of my enemies. You anoint my head with oil; my cup overflows.

Psalm 23:5

DECEMBER 23

Morning: Fear the LORD, you his saints, for those who fear him lack nothing.

Psalm 34:9

Evening: How good and pleasant it is when brothers live together in unity!

Psalm 133:1

DECEMBER 24

Morning: But my eyes are fixed on you, O Sovereign LORD; in you I take refuge—do not give me over to death.

Psalm 141:8

Evening: But it is God who judges: He brings one down, he exalts another.

Psalm 75:7

DECEMBER 25

Morning: Who is he, this King of glory? The LORD Almighty—he is the King of glory. Selah

Psalm 24:10

Evening: Let them praise the name of the LORD, for his name alone is exalted; his splendor is above the earth and the heavens.

Psalm 148:13

DECEMBER 26

Morning: Blessed are the people of whom this is true; blessed are the people whose God is the LORD.

Psalm 144:15

Evening: O LORD, do not rebuke me in your anger or discipline me in your wrath.

Psalm 6:1

DECEMBER 27

Morning: Continue your love to those who know you, your righteousness to the upright in heart.

Psalm 36:10

Evening: I remember the days of long ago; I meditate on all your works and consider what your hands have done.

Psalm 143:5

DECEMBER 28

Morning: My mouth will speak in praise of the LORD. Let every creature praise his holy name for ever and ever.

Psalm 145:21

Evening: You know when I sit and when I rise; you perceive my thoughts from afar.

Psalm 139:2

DECEMBER 29

Morning: All mankind will fear; they will proclaim the works of God and ponder what he has done.

Psalm 64:9

Evening: May the arrogant be put to shame for wronging me without cause; but I will meditate on your precepts.

Psalm 119:78

DECEMBER 30

Morning: Praise him, sun and moon, praise him, all you shining stars.

Psalm 148:3

Evening: He determines the number of the stars and calls them each by name.

Psalm 147:4

DECEMBER 31

Morning: I have hidden your word in my heart that I might not sin against you.

Psalm 119:11

Evening: The LORD will watch over your coming and going both now and forevermore.

Psalm 121:8